EARTH

JEN GREEN

COPPER BEECH BOOKS • BROOKFIELD, CONNECTICUT

© Aladdin Books Ltd 1998
Designed and produced by
Aladdin Books Ltd
28 Percy Street
London W1P 0LD

First published in the United States in 1998 by
Copper Beech Books,
an imprint of
The Millbrook Press
2 Old New Milford Road
Brookfield, Connecticut 06804

Printed in Belgium

Editor
Simon Beecroft
Design
David West
Children's Book Design
Designer
Robert Perry
Illustrators
Richard Rockwood
& Ian Thompson
Picture Research
Brooks Krikler Research

A copy of the CIP data is kept on record
at the Library of Congress.
ISBN 0-7613-0856-3 (lib. bdg.)

CONTENTS

Introduction

"The earth was trembling. I saw the mountain slide toward the village and said, 'I am ready to die'." *Eyewitness, Iran earthquake, 1990*

The ground under our feet may feel "rock-solid," but it is not. Earthquakes can shake the ground, and landslides and avalanches can sweep the land away. When the ground splits open, or molten rock from inside the earth spews out onto the surface, buildings and forests fall like bowling pins. The earth's movements are beyond our control. All we can do is monitor them, try to predict where disasters will strike, and equip our emergency services to deal with them.

Our planet is not solid all the way through, but is made up of different layers (*above*). Below the

Crust
Upper mantle
Lower mantle
Outer core
Inner core

hard outer crust lies the rocky mantle, in which there is a layer of soft, squishy rock. The rest of the mantle is solid, and below this lies the superhot core, made of iron. The outer core is liquid and the inner core is compressed to a solid.

The earth's crust itself is not a continuous layer. It is made up of sections called tectonic plates, which fit together like pieces of a giant jigsaw. The plates float on the soft layer in the upper mantle like huge rafts.

Earthquakes and volcanoes (*below*) are common along the edges of the earth's tectonic plates.

Pangaea

200 million years ago

EARTH MYTHS

Myths and legends around the world reflect the shifting, unstable nature of the earth's surface. Some ancient peoples pictured the earth as supported by a giant beast or beasts. In Hindu myth, for example, the earth is carried on the back of elephants, which are standing on a turtle (right). The turtle in turn is balanced on a cobra! When any of the animals move, the earth may quiver and shake, causing earthquakes or volcanoes.

Oldest known rocks   First living cells   Blue-green algae   Green algae

4 billion years ago   3 billion years ago   2 billion years ago   1 billion years ago

First solid crust   Continents and oceans formed

100 million years ago

50 million years ago

SHAPING THE EARTH

The earth's surface has not always looked the way it does today. During its earliest days, about 4 billion years ago, the earth was a hot, waterless planet (above). The planet became a suitable place for life to evolve about 3.5 billion years ago.

The continents drifted together to form a single landmass called Pangaea about 200 million years ago (left). Over millions of years, plates carrying the continents slowly drifted apart, to form the lands and seas we know today.

Present day

DRIFTING PLATES

The plates that form the earth's crust are still drifting. They move only very slowly, at a rate of between 0.8 and 8 in (2–20 cm) each year. The Red Sea, below the Sinai Peninsula in the Middle East (right), is being widened by about 0.5 in (1 cm) a year as plates beneath drift apart.

When an oceanic plate collides with a continental plate, the oceanic plate is pushed down below the other. The ocean crust melts deep inside the earth, and then is forced up again through the continental plate, to form ranges of volcanic mountains near the continent's edge.

The Rocky Mountains, in western North America (right), were formed this way, by a massive collision between the Pacific and the North American plates.

Mountain-building

"Like a living thing, Earth is in constant motion."
Geologist, United States, 1998

The earth's landscapes, and mountains in particular, are formed by movements of the earth's tectonic plates. Driven by currents deep in the mantle, the plates may collide, drift apart, or rub against one another. Volcanoes and geological upheaval are the result. Plates may be carrying oceans or continents, or parts of each. The effects of plate collisions vary, depending on whether they happen on land or at sea (*see* page 7).

Where the earth's crust is weak, often along plate edges, magma (molten rock) may force its way up to the surface. Red-hot lava and ash spill out and build up around the opening to form a volcano. Clouds of boiling gas and steam shoot high into the air. When this happens under the sea, an underwater volcanic mountain may appear. This is how, in 1963, the island of Surtsey, just south of Iceland, was formed.

The island of Surtsey is the top of an underwater volcanic mountain (*above*).

BLOCK MOUNTAINS

Faults are cracks that occur between two plates, where the earth has shifted. The land on either side of the fault may be forced upward or slip downward, to form block mountains (right). Where faults run parallel to one another, as they do in eastern Africa (above), the land in between may subside to form a rift valley edged by mountains.

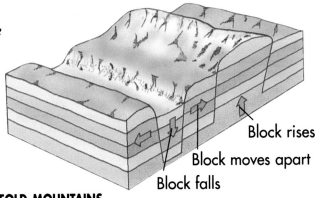

Block rises

Block moves apart

Block falls

FOLD MOUNTAINS

When two continental plates collide, neither dives below the other. Instead, tremendous pressure forces the crust upward. Layers of rock are bent and crumpled into jagged ranges called fold mountains (below). The Alps (left) are an example of this type of mountain-building.

Plate

Rock folds under pressure

TOO MUCH PRESSURE

Earthquakes are caused by plates moving against each other (right). Rocks along a fault line may absorb the pressure of plate movements deep inside the earth for many years. Suddenly, the tension is released as the plates snap into a new position along a fault. The energy is released in a series of seismic (shock) waves, which radiate out from the earthquake's center (the focus). The most devastated area is the epicenter, the area on the surface above the focus.

1 Two tectonic plates slide against each other.

Fault line

2 The movement of the plates causes stress to build up, stretching the rock.

3 As the rock snaps into a new position, an earthquake is produced.

Focus

Seismic waves

REDUCED TO RUBBLE

Minor tremors can give a warning of a larger earthquake to come. The ground may shake gently, and swell and crack as rocks beneath begin to warp and bulge. Major earthquakes cause almost instant devastation. Within seconds, buildings collapse with a roar as the ground beneath them splits and heaves. In 1989, the San Francisco earthquake brought buildings crashing to the ground. In one tragic incident, a concrete highway collapsed, crushing 42 people.

A crack opens up along a road during the San Francisco earthquake of 1989 (*above*).

Quaking Earth

"There was a loud humming noise, then steam burst out of the ground. It was as if the earth was boiling." *Survivor, Armenian earthquake, 1988*

Earthquakes strike with little or no warning. Within seconds, they can shatter whole cities and cause great loss of life. Earthquakes are caused by sudden movements of tectonic plates (*see* page 8). Minor quakes may precede the main quake, and aftershocks may follow it. The vibrations cause buildings to sway and fall, hillsides to crumble, roads to crack — even railroad tracks to bend (*above*).

One of the most notorious fault lines in the world is the San Andreas Fault in California (*below*). It runs from the city of San Francisco along the coast of California to Mexico. Here, the Pacific Plate is slowly drifting northwestward, grinding up against the North American Plate.

Since 1906, when San Francisco was devastated by a violent earthquake, scientists have kept a careful watch on earth movements in the region, hoping to predict when the next major earthquake would happen.

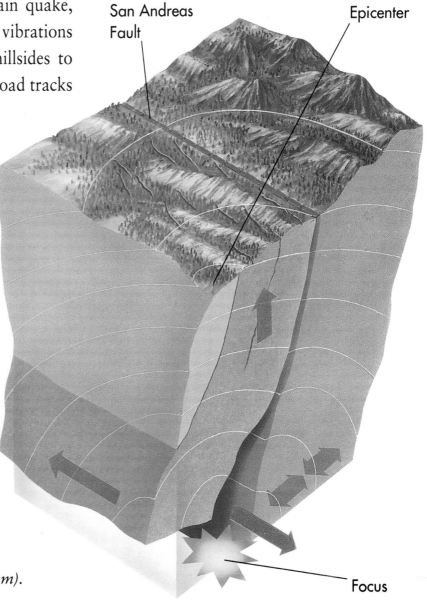

San Andreas Fault

Epicenter

Focus

SHOCK WAVES

In 1989, a large quake occurred directly below the Santa Cruz Mountains (right) along the San Andreas Fault. As the Pacific Plate jerked forward and upward, shock waves were sent out across an area of 600,000 square miles (1.6 million sq km).

Fires rage through a town on the island of Okushiri in northern Japan after an earthquake (*above*).

Aftermath of an earthquake

"I rushed to the front door, sure the house would fall. It rocked like a ship on a rough sea." *Eyewitness, San Francisco earthquake, 1906*

Most earthquakes last for less than a minute. The longest quake ever recorded, which shook the port of Anchorage in Alaska in 1964, still lasted only four minutes. But the earthquake itself is only the start of the destruction. Fires break out as electricity and gas supply lines are ripped apart.

When water supplies are also severed, fires can be very difficult to put out. In 1995, the city of Kobe in Japan was devastated by fires caused by broken gas mains following a massive earthquake.

Earth tremors beneath the ocean cause *tsunamis*, giant waves that sweep ashore, flooding towns and villages along the coast. In 1755, the port of Lisbon in Portugal was lashed by massive shock waves and *tsunamis* (*left*) after an undersea quake, causing the deaths of 60,000 people. Dams and reservoirs on land nearby may crack and burst, also leading to flooding. The destruction is often greatest on soft ground, where shock waves cause soft soil to turn to liquid, toppling buildings.

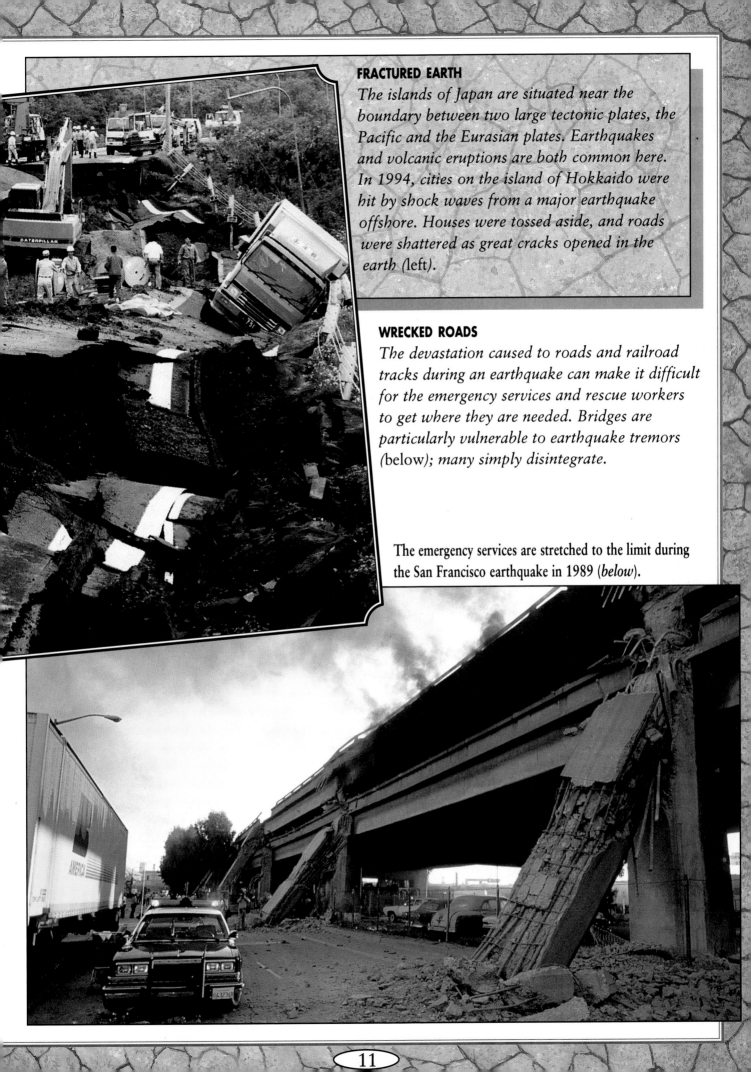

FRACTURED EARTH

The islands of Japan are situated near the boundary between two large tectonic plates, the Pacific and the Eurasian plates. Earthquakes and volcanic eruptions are both common here. In 1994, cities on the island of Hokkaido were hit by shock waves from a major earthquake offshore. Houses were tossed aside, and roads were shattered as great cracks opened in the earth (left).

WRECKED ROADS

The devastation caused to roads and railroad tracks during an earthquake can make it difficult for the emergency services and rescue workers to get where they are needed. Bridges are particularly vulnerable to earthquake tremors (below); many simply disintegrate.

The emergency services are stretched to the limit during the San Francisco earthquake in 1989 (*below*).

To the rescue

"We may only be able to reach the survivors by helicopter."
Relief worker, Afghanistan earthquake, June 1998

After an earthquake, the rescue services swing into action as soon as possible. It is a race against time to locate survivors. Emergency services face many difficulties in the stricken area. Roads and railroads are often wrecked, making it difficult to even reach the disaster zone. Supplies, equipment, and rescue teams must all be ferried in by helicopter. If electricity lines are down, power tools need their own generators to work. In remote areas, vital earthmoving equipment such as cranes and bulldozers may be in short supply.

The first priority of the emergency services is to save as many lives as possible. Medical staff tend victims pulled from the rubble (*left*), as rescue teams go back to search for others. Food and shelter are needed for people made homeless through the disaster. After the survivors have been rescued, all power supplies must be made safe, to protect against fire. Water supplies must also be restored, or disease will spread. Once the danger is over, the work of clearing the rubble of ruined buildings begins. Only then can people return and start to rebuild their lives.

SEARCHING FOR SURVIVORS

When an earthquake struck the remote Republic of Armenia, part of the former Soviet Union, in December 1988, rescue efforts were hampered by the harsh winter weather. Many countries sent food, clothing, medical supplies, and rescue teams to help. Rescuers searched with sniffer dogs for survivors buried in the wreckage (left), or used thermal image cameras, which can detect body heat.

A rescuer with a sniffer dog searches for survivors after an earthquake in Armenia, 1988.

BLAZING INFERNO

Fire is a major hazard after earthquakes. After the 1989 earthquake in San Francisco, hundreds of fires raged throughout the city (above), including a major fuel spill at the city's airport. Three hundred off-duty firefighters, more than twice the city's usual number, were called in to help. Firefighting is made particularly difficult when water supplies are severed after a quake.

CLEARING THE WRECKAGE

When earthquakes hit Mexico City in 1985, hundreds of buildings were destroyed (right). One hospital collapsed story by story, killing 1,000 people. Rescue workers were hindered by a lack of earthmoving equipment to help clear the wreckage. Amazingly, a tiny baby was lifted from the ruins unharmed, after spending nine days buried under rubble.

SHATTERED EARTH

In February and May 1998, large earthquakes hit the remote, mountainous country of Afghanistan in southwestern Asia (above). International rescue teams helped set up emergency shelters to house and feed survivors and give medical help.

THE 'FRISCO QUAKE

The San Francisco earthquake of 1906 is one of the most infamous disasters in history (right). One eyewitness reported: "The street seemed to move like waves of water. I was covered and blinded by the dust." Factories, theaters, and houses in the city center collapsed, and fire ravaged the buildings that remained. In all, 700 people died, and thousands were made homeless.

Mexico City, the capital of Mexico, is built on the soft sand and gravel of a drained lake bed. During the 1985 earthquake, the soft soil collapsed, and buildings fell like bowling pins (right). More than 8,000 people died in the disaster, and the extensive damage came to a total of $5 billion.

Famous quakes

"People shouted 'Run, run, the building will fall,' but we didn't know where to run." *Survivor, Mexico City earthquake, 1985*

Somewhere in the world every minute, the earth shakes. Most tremors are too small to be noticed, but every year, about 1,000 quakes cause damage. Now and then a major earthquake strikes.

China has had more than its share of large earthquakes. The most deadly quake ever recorded struck the province of Shensi in 1556. Between 800,000 and a million people died — by far the largest death toll in history. In 1976, the deadliest quake of modern times struck the highly populated city of Tangshan, east of Beijing. A network of coal-mining tunnels under the city collapsed, and few buildings were left standing. At least 240,000 people died.

The Armenian earthquake of 1988 was one of the largest in living memory. The town of Spitak was utterly destroyed. The only protection against the severe winter weather were flimsy tents and makeshift shelters (*above*).

Train services are delayed after the earthquake in Tangshan, China, in 1976 (*right*).

THROWN OFF TRACK

When Tangshan in China was laid waste by the earthquake of 1976, trains and cars were tossed from railroad tracks (right). The railroad network around the city was so badly damaged that 144 miles (230 km) of track had to be replaced.

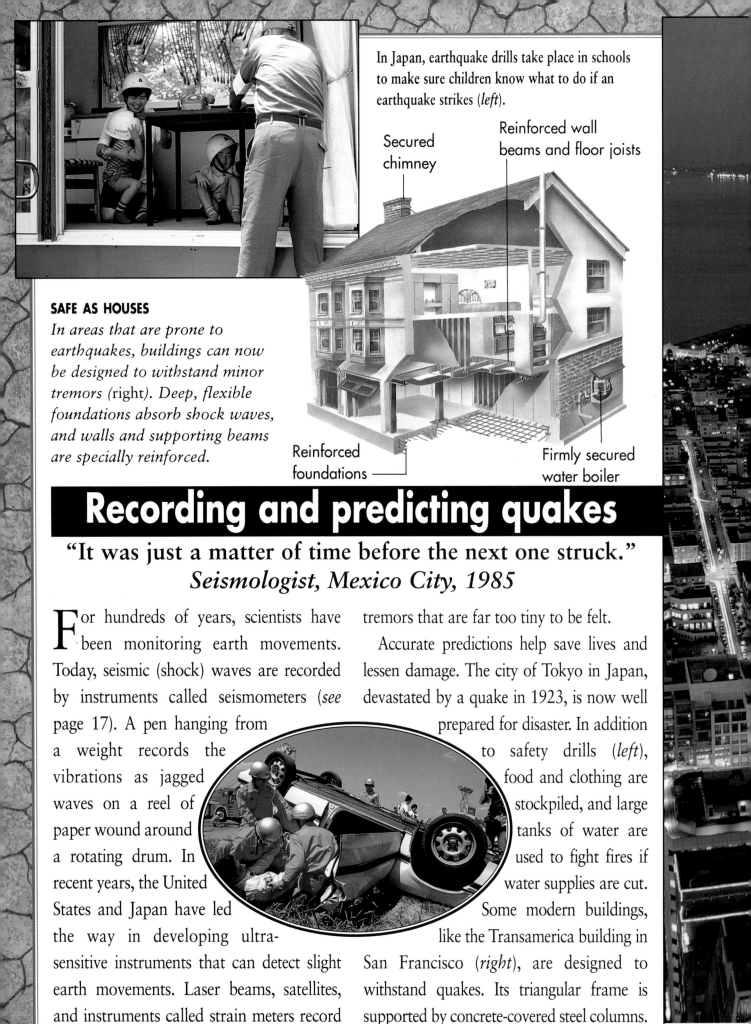

In Japan, earthquake drills take place in schools to make sure children know what to do if an earthquake strikes (*left*).

Secured chimney

Reinforced wall beams and floor joists

SAFE AS HOUSES

In areas that are prone to earthquakes, buildings can now be designed to withstand minor tremors (right). Deep, flexible foundations absorb shock waves, and walls and supporting beams are specially reinforced.

Reinforced foundations

Firmly secured water boiler

Recording and predicting quakes

"It was just a matter of time before the next one struck."
Seismologist, Mexico City, 1985

For hundreds of years, scientists have been monitoring earth movements. Today, seismic (shock) waves are recorded by instruments called seismometers (*see page 17*). A pen hanging from a weight records the vibrations as jagged waves on a reel of paper wound around a rotating drum. In recent years, the United States and Japan have led the way in developing ultra-sensitive instruments that can detect slight earth movements. Laser beams, satellites, and instruments called strain meters record tremors that are far too tiny to be felt.

Accurate predictions help save lives and lessen damage. The city of Tokyo in Japan, devastated by a quake in 1923, is now well prepared for disaster. In addition to safety drills (*left*), food and clothing are stockpiled, and large tanks of water are used to fight fires if water supplies are cut. Some modern buildings, like the Transamerica building in San Francisco (*right*), are designed to withstand quakes. Its triangular frame is supported by concrete-covered steel columns.

EARLY SEISMOMETER

The earliest instrument for detecting seismic waves was invented in China in the 2nd century AD. A pendulum hung inside a bronze vessel, with dragon heads around the rim (above). When the earth shook, the vessel moved, and a bronze ball dropped from a dragon's head into an open-mouthed toad below. Modern seismometers (below) are more sophisticated, but work on the same principle.

MEASURING QUAKES

Two scales are used to measure seismic activity. Most often used today, the Richter Scale calculates the strength of quakes from seismograph readings. As an alternative, the Mercalli Scale (below) measures the intensity of earthquakes by the damage they cause.

12 Total destruction

1 Tiny tremor

The Mercalli system grades earth tremors on a scale from 1 to 12 (above).

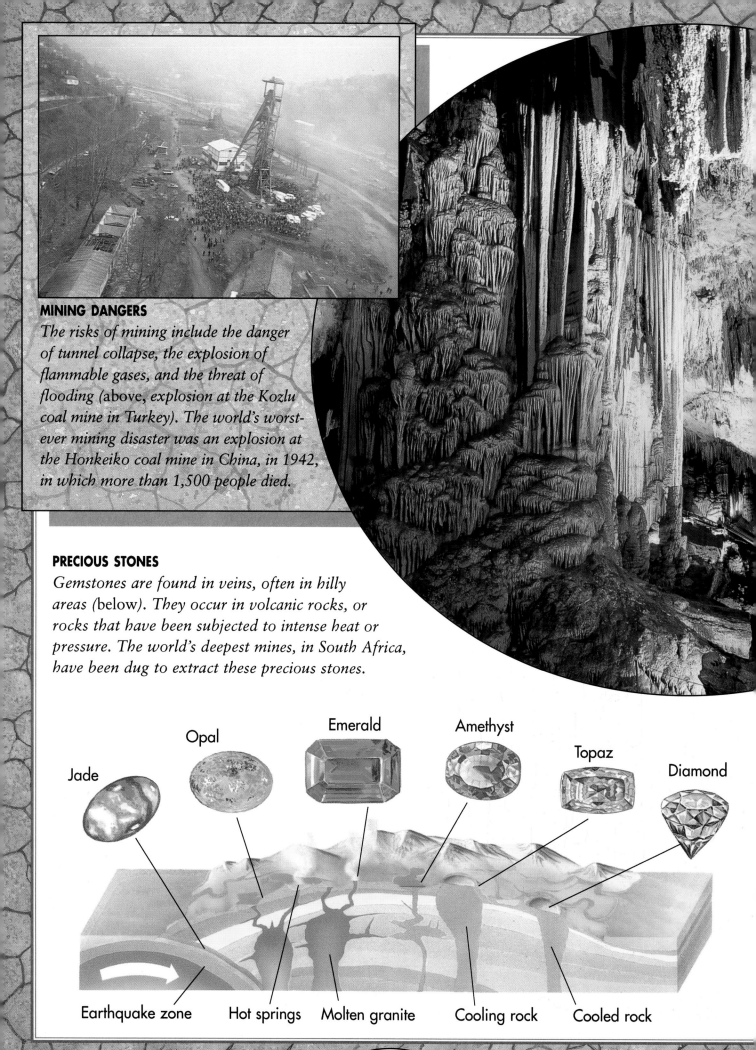

MINING DANGERS

The risks of mining include the danger of tunnel collapse, the explosion of flammable gases, and the threat of flooding (above, explosion at the Kozlu coal mine in Turkey). The world's worst-ever mining disaster was an explosion at the Honkeiko coal mine in China, in 1942, in which more than 1,500 people died.

PRECIOUS STONES

Gemstones are found in veins, often in hilly areas (below). They occur in volcanic rocks, or rocks that have been subjected to intense heat or pressure. The world's deepest mines, in South Africa, have been dug to extract these precious stones.

Jade

Opal

Emerald

Amethyst

Topaz

Diamond

Earthquake zone   Hot springs   Molten granite   Cooling rock   Cooled rock

Into the earth

"Mines are like any other modern factory. But the job is still dirty, hard, and dangerous." *Miner, Britain, 1998*

The earth is a rich natural resource that provides many materials vital to our daily lives. Rocks are the building blocks of the earth. They are made from minerals, chemical substances that form naturally in the earth. The earth's crust is made up of about 3,000 different minerals. Some are valuable, or useful to us in other ways. Mineral ores contain metals such as iron and copper. Gemstones such as diamonds and rubies are prized for their great beauty. Coal, oil, and natural gas are fuels that provide us with energy. Rocks such as sandstone, granite, and slate make good building materials. Other rocks contain useful chemicals, like sulfur and asbestos, which are used in industry.

The earth's useful minerals can be extracted in various ways. Minerals found near the surface are mined by removing surface rock (*above*). Shafts and tunnels are dug or blasted to mine deposits deeper underground. Wells are sunk to extract reserves of oil and gas.

Limestone rock is made from the mineral calcite, which is soluble in acidic groundwater and can form caves (*left*).

VALUABLE METALS

Most metals are found as ores, mixed in with other substances. Gold and platinum are metals that occur in a pure form. Here, miners blast platinum from the surrounding rock with pneumatic drills.

Mining is hot, dirty, dangerous work. In the 20th century, improved technology and new regulations have helped make mines safer places to work, but despite all the precautions, disasters still occur.

Thick black soil   Red soil   Desert soil   Arid soil   Peaty soil

There are different kinds of soil, from loose sand to heavy peat (*left*). Different soils have various colors and textures, depending on the minerals they contain. Different crops do best in certain soils.

Farming the soil

"Since the 1950s, demand for food throughout the world has more than doubled, putting increased pressure on farmers." *U.S. Official, 1992*

If you scoop up a handful of soil, you will be holding one of Earth's richest resources. All life on Earth depends on the soil for food, either directly or indirectly. Plants draw nutrients (nourishment) from the soil to grow. Animals feed on plants, or on the animals that feed on them. Pesticides and fertilizers are sprayed onto crops to help them grow (*above*).

The soil is made up of different layers. On the top is a rich, dark layer of humus, made up of rotting plants. The topsoil contains decaying remains of plants and animals, which are broken down by burrowing creatures such as insects and worms, and by minute bacteria and fungi. Below the topsoil, the subsoil contains fewer plant and animal remains, and more pieces of rock. Solid bedrock lies beneath the soil.

Soil is formed as rock is broken down (eroded) by ice, frost, and wind. Soil takes hundreds, even thousands of years to form. But it can be destroyed in a fraction of the time, by bad farming methods, or by extreme weather conditions (*below*).

Overgrazing by domestic herds.

Cash crops replace local food crops.

Trees cut down for fuel.

Vegetation burned to make grazing land for cattle.

Domestic and wild animals compete for drinking water.

Rivers dry up because of the lack of rainfall.

Bad farming practices (*left*) range from overgrazing to cutting down too many trees, which causes soil to fall apart. Natural hazards include lack of rainfall (drought) and extreme winds.

VITAL FOOD

More than half of the world's food comes from just three crops — wheat, maize (corn), and rice, the last of which is grown in flooded fields called paddies (above). Huge areas of land are given over to growing just one of these crops, a practice that is known as monoculture. But growing just one crop can exhaust the soil, and can be risky. If the crop fails due to bad weather, plant disease, or insect infestation, there could be poor harvests for a number of years.

A tractor plows the heavy soil of northern Europe (*left*).

DUSTBOWL DAYS

The soil suffers when land is overgrazed by animals, or when crops are farmed too intensively. When the natural vegetation is removed, soil is no longer protected against wind and rain. In the American Midwest in the 1930s, farmers plowed up vast areas for wheat, removing the native grasses that had anchored the soil. Drought turned the soil to dust, and high winds carried it away, creating the "Dust Bowl" (right). It took many years of careful management before the land became fertile again.

Landslides

"There was a loud roar. Our homes were wiped out in seconds." *Survivor, Vaiont Dam disaster, 1963*

Rockslide

Landslides and rockfalls occur where the soil becomes unstable. Natural weathering or heavy rainfall may be the cause. After torrential rain, soil layers can get waterlogged and slippery, and may start to slide away. In many areas, tree and plant roots anchor the soil and help hold it together. On steep slopes, landslides occur where the soil is loose because trees have been cut down. Quarrying and mining can also lead to landslides. Where large amounts of rock have been removed, the land may be undercut and start to crumble away. Some landslides and rockfalls are caused by earthquakes.

When a landslide begins, large boulders and smaller fragments bounce and crash downhill. Gravity takes over, and the rocks gather speed. On steep ground, the landslide soon becomes unstoppable. Forests and settlements in its path are buried or swept away.

In May 1998, a massive earthquake in Afghanistan caused an entire mountainside to collapse. The resulting landslides blocked rivers and streams, and led to extensive flooding.

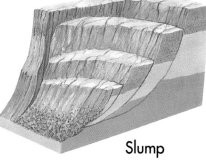

Rockfall

Slump

Rockslides involve the downward movement of large blocks of rock (*top*). Rockfalls occur when rocks fall down a steep slope or cliff face (*middle*). Slumps occur when heavy rock and soil collapse in a series of curving movements (*bottom*).

CINDER SLIDE

Landslides can be caused by spoil heaps — piles of soil or rock left over by the mining industry. In Japan in 1965, a hill of cinders perched high above Kawasaki, near Tokyo, became unstable after heavy rain. Rock and cinders slid down onto the village, killing 24 people. More than 600 rescue workers dug to release people buried in the debris (left).

Landslide caused by the wearing away of the lower slopes of a valley by a river (*below*).

Direction of landslide

Water-soaked rocks

DAMBUSTER

One of the world's worst landslide disasters occurred in Italy, in 1963. Above a well-populated valley, the river Piave had been dammed to create the Vaiont Reservoir. Heavy rains caused the mountainsides to collapse into the reservoir. A mass of water surged over the top of the dam and cascaded down into the valley below. Several villages were wiped out. More than 2,600 people died, and only the church steeple of Longarone was left standing (above).

COLLAPSING CLIFFS

In coastal areas, the pounding of the wind and waves can cause cliffs to collapse. Houses built at a safe distance from the cliff may suddenly find themselves on the very edge (right). In a few more years, winter storms may bring them crashing to the beach, or they may simply be abandoned by frightened owners.

DEADLY TIDE

In California in 1969, torrential rains brought down a flood of mud and gravel from the San Gabriel Mountains (right). A roaring tide swept down the mountain, carrying huge boulders and uprooting tree trunks in its wake. The river of mud cascaded through the suburb of Glendora, on the outskirts of Los Angeles, and 100 people drowned.

Direction of
mud flow

ABERFAN DISASTER

In 1966, tragedy struck the village of Aberfan in southern Wales when a large pile of coal-mining waste perched above the village collapsed after heavy rain. A tide of wet sludge engulfed part of the village and the local school, and 145 people, including 116 children, died.

Glendora

VOLCANIC FLOW

In 1991, the eruption of Mt. Pinatubo in the Philippines sent huge clouds of ash into the air. A thick layer of ash settled on towns and villages around the mountain, burying trees and houses (right). Soon after, heavy rains turned the ash into deadly mudflows, which smothered villages and smashed through roads and bridges.

Mudflows

"The mountain opened up in five places and a sea of mud poured down like lava." *Rescue worker, southern Italy, 1998*

Where landslides are caused by heavy rain, the result may be a deadly river of mud. With a texture like wet cement, mudflows can travel at great speed and spread over a wide area (*right*). In southern Italy, in 1998, heavy rain caused mountain rivers to flood, loosening rocks and boulders. A roaring tide of mud and rocks swept through low-lying villages. In some areas, mud was 7 feet (2 meters) deep, and 3,000 people had to be moved out.

Other deadly mudflows, called *lahars*, are triggered by erupting volcanoes, which cause rivers of ash, melting snow, and ice to spill down from above. In 1985, a volcano called Nevado del Ruiz in Colombia erupted, spewing large quantities of hot ash onto high, snow-covered slopes. The snow melted, and a tide of mud raced down the mountain, engulfing the town of Armero in the valley below. More than 23,000 people were killed by the deadly flow. Rescuers could not approach the disaster zone on foot, for fear of sinking in the mud, and the only way of rescuing survivors was by helicopter.

LETHAL FLOW

Mudflows occur in mountainous regions, desert areas, and on steep-sided volcanoes. They occur after heavy rains and can travel at speeds of up to 55 mph (88 km/h, right).

Large tongue of mud, water, and fine debris

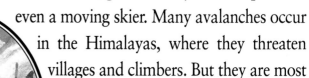

Avalanche!

"We saw a cloud of snow and ice flying downward, with a roar like that of ten thousand wild beasts." *Survivor, Mt. Huascarán avalanche, 1962*

An avalanche is a mass of ice and snow that breaks away from a mountain to crash down at high speed. The most dangerous kind, dry-snow avalanches, can race along at up to 185 mph (300 km/h). Avalanches are often triggered by heavy snowfalls, particularly during the spring, when melting snow creates a slippery layer on which new snowfalls can slide. They may also be set off by shockwaves from an earthquake, or by much smaller vibrations, produced by a small plane or even a moving skier. Many avalanches occur in the Himalayas, where they threaten villages and climbers. But they are most deadly in the highly populated Alps.

Being caught in an avalanche is a truly terrifying experience. Victims may be catapulted down steep slopes or buried alive. Trapped under snow (*left*), survivors find it difficult to breathe or move, or even tell which way up they are. Rescuers must come quickly, by helicopter and with trained sniffer dogs, or victims will die from their injuries, or from cold or suffocation.

The movie *Cliffhanger* (1993, *below*) showed the terrifying nature of avalanches.

SHATTERED HOUSES

Avalanches pose a threat to settlements on steep, snowy slopes. Houses are crushed or swept away (above). One survivor saw his village wiped out in seconds. He reported: "When I regained my senses, I saw only a waste of mud and ice."

WINTER OF TERROR

The Alps have a long history of deadly avalanches. In 1950-51, a series of avalanches swept through Alpine villages and killed a total of 240 people. In Switzerland, the village of Vals (right) was cut in two by a torrent of ice, rocks, and snow. In January 1998, 11 hikers were killed when their movements set off an avalanche 7,590 ft (2,300 m) up the French Alps.

WALL OF ICE

One of the worst avalanche disasters occured in Peru in 1962 (right). It began after bright sunshine had melted ice fields high on the snowy peak of Mt. Huascarán. Ice and snow broke off a high glacier and thundered down the mountain. A tide of ice, rocks, and boulders engulfed villages in the foothills, and 3,500 people died.

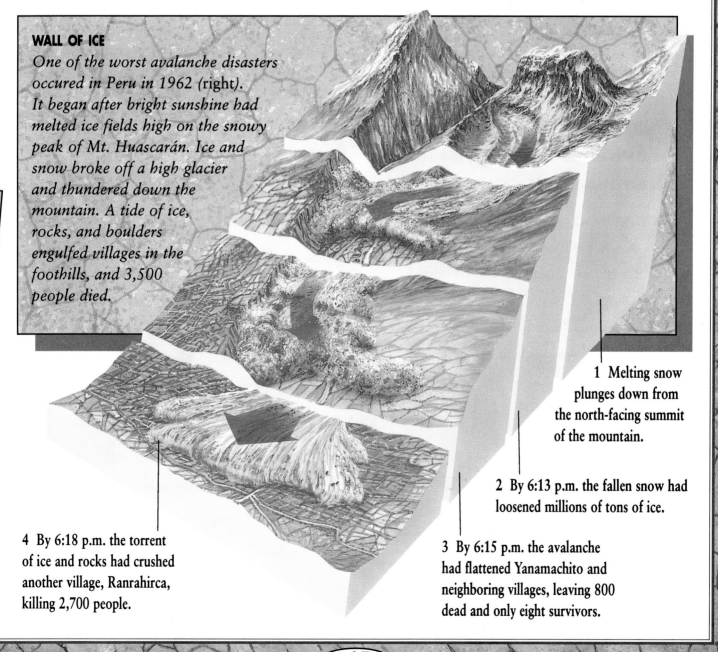

1 Melting snow plunges down from the north-facing summit of the mountain.

2 By 6:13 p.m. the fallen snow had loosened millions of tons of ice.

3 By 6:15 p.m. the avalanche had flattened Yanamachito and neighboring villages, leaving 800 dead and only eight survivors.

4 By 6:18 p.m. the torrent of ice and rocks had crushed another village, Ranrahirca, killing 2,700 people.

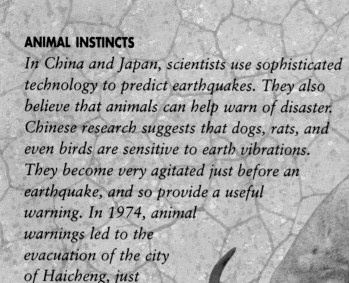

Bizarre Earth

"Everyone thought that the end of the world was approaching." *Witness to a meteorite fall, Siberia, 1908*

Since the dawn of history, people have lived in awe of the earth's natural forces. Earthquakes, volcanoes, and landslides were interpreted as signs of the anger of the gods.

Similarly, unusual features in the landscape were viewed with awe and wonder. Towering peaks, bizarre rock pinnacles, and mighty waterfalls were seen as dwelling places of gods and spirits. Sacred ceremonies took place at giant outcrops such as Uluru (Ayer's Rock) in Australia (*see* page 29). Myths and legends explained how natural wonders such as this were formed.

Today, we understand much more about the origins of our planet, and how many of the other bizarre features of the earth's landscape were formed. We happily bathe in mineral-rich mud that has been warmed by underground volcanic heat (*left*) — and yet, despite the range of sophisticated technology used today, we are not able to control entirely the earth's natural forces. We are still in awe of the force and power of our planet.

This giant bowl shape, in Arizona (*right*), was not created by any natural force from Earth, but by a missile from outer space. It is the impact crater of a giant meteorite that smashed onto the surface of our planet about 22,000 years ago.

MAGIC ROCK

Uluru, also known as Ayer's Rock, is a giant mass of sandstone found in the middle of a great, flat desert in Australia (left). To the Aborigines, it is a sacred place. Detailed paintings decorate the walls of sacred caves at the base of the rock.

NATURAL SCULPTURES

Wind and waves are powerful forces that can carve solid rock into weird and wonderful shapes. Here, waves have worn away the softer rock of the cliffs to make a natural arch (right). At some time in the future, the arch will collapse to form freestanding rock pillars, called sea stacks.

Emergency first aid

If you hear an earthquake warning:

• Move heavy objects off high shelves.

• Prepare emergency supplies of fresh water, food, a flashlight, first aid kit, and fire extinguisher.

• Tune to a local radio station and listen for reports and instructions.

• Turn off supplies of gas, water, and electricity if you are told to do so.

If an earthquake is imminent:

• If you are indoors, stay away from windows.

• Go down to a basement or lower floor if there is one, but do not enter an elevator to do so.

• Get under a strong desk or table.

• If you are outside, flat ground or even a hilltop is safer than a steep slope, which may start to slide.

• Keep well away from tall buildings and trees.

• Lie flat on the ground and do not try to run.

After an earthquake:

• Check yourself and others for injuries and apply first aid with the help of a first aid guide.

• Get the injured to the hospital as soon as possible.

• Do not enter damaged buildings.

• Boil and filter all drinking water.

• Do not light fires if there is the risk of a gas leak.

If you are caught in an avalanche:

• Remove heavy kit such as backpacks.

• IMPORTANT: Cover your nose and mouth to avoid swallowing snow.

• Use a swimming stroke to try to keep to the top of the fall.

• When the avalanche comes to rest, make as big a space around your body as you can.

• Try to reach the surface if possible. Otherwise, save your energy to call out once you hear rescuers.

Glossary

Avalanche A falling mass of ice, snow, and rock.

Core The super-hot center of the earth, made of iron. The outer part of the core is liquid and the inner part is compressed into a solid.

Crust The hard, outer layer of the earth.

Earthquake A violent shaking of the earth's crust, caused by movements inside the earth.

Elements The basic building blocks of everything on Earth. There were once thought to be just four elements: air, earth, fire, and water.

Epicenter The point on the earth's surface directly above the focus of an earthquake.

Erosion The wearing away of the land by natural forces including ice, frost, wind, and running water. Human activities such as mining and tree-felling can also lead to erosion.

Fault A crack or break in the rocks that form Earth's surface, where rocks can slide against one another.

Fertilizer A chemical substance that nourishes plants and helps them to grow.

Focus The point inside the earth where pressure is released during an earthquake.

Lahar A flow of melting ice and snow, rocks, and ash or lava from an erupting volcano.

Lava Molten rock from inside the earth that erupts onto the surface.

Magma Molten rock inside the earth.

Mantle The semimolten layer of rock inside the earth, between the crust and the central core.

Mercalli scale Method of recording the strength of an earthquake by its effects on the surrounding area, specifically the level of damage caused.

Minerals Chemical substances found in the earth's crust.

Ore A mineral that contains a valuable substance such as a metal.

Pesticides Chemicals that are used to destroy pests, including insects, that harm plants.

Richter scale Method of recording the strength of an earthquake based on the energy released.

Seismic wave A burst of energy produced underground by an earthquake. When seismic waves reach the surface, they cause the ground to shake. Seismic waves are also known as shock waves.

Seismometer An instrument for measuring seismic waves.

Strain meter An instrument used to detect movements in the earth's crust.

Tectonic plate One of the giant slabs of rock that make up the earth's crust. The earth's tectonic plates are constantly moving.

Tremor A violent trembling of the ground that precedes and follows an earthquake.

Tsunami A giant sea wave caused by an earthquake on the seabed. Tsunamis are also known as tidal waves, although they are not caused by tides.

Index

Picture Credits

(t-top, m-middle, b-bottom, r-right, l-left)

Front cover all, 5b, 6b, 8, 9t, 10t, 11 both, 12 both, 13 both, 14t, 15t & m, 16 both, 17r, 18l, 19t, 20, 21t, 23b, 25t, 28t, & 30 — Frank Spooner Pictures. 2-3, 7t, 17l, 18-19, 19b, 29t & m — Pictor International. 4, 7b, & 9b — Spectrum Color Library. 5t, 10b, & 14b — Mary Evans Picture Library. 6t & 29b — Roger Vlitos. 15b, 21b, 22, 23t, 24, 25b, 26r, 27, & 31 — Hulton Getty Collection. 21m – Eye Ubiquitous. 26l — Tristar Pictures (courtesy Kobal)